ALSO BY RYAN KIDD

"These Memories I Leave to You"
by Ryan Kidd and Dave Scott

"The Newcomers"
by Ryan Kidd

Intriguing Port Sydney Stories & Photos

RYAN KIDD

Order this book online at www.trafford.com
or email orders@trafford.com

Most Trafford titles are also available at major online book retailers.

Print information available on the last page.

ISBN: 978-1-6987-0251-3 (sc)
ISBN: 978-1-6987-0250-6 (hc)
ISBN: 978-1-6987-0249-0 (e)

Library of Congress Control Number: 2020913839

Trafford rev. 07/27/2020

North America & international
toll-free: 1 888 232 4444 (USA & Canada)
fax: 812 355 4082

Intriguing Port Sydney Stories & Pictures

The people of Port Sydney and Mary Lake upon which it is located were unique. They arrived with the first rush of settlers. They were also well educated and were "characters". Yes the area followed the usual pattern ...lumbering, the era of the lodges and eventually cottagers and their supporting trades....but the community left its indelible mark in its development because of these unique people. I hope that I have been able to demonstrate this in the book.

This book is meant to follow the other two books: 'These Memories I Leave to You and the Newcomers"

The selection of material is thus limited to:

What is available.

What has not been dealt with in these previous books.

I hope that you enjoy the stories.

DEDICATION

....to the Pioneers who through their dreams, inspiration, and hard work made Port Sydney into the fine community that we cherish today ....

CONTENTS

Dedication vii

Chapter One 1

Chapter Two 13

Chapter Three 25

Chapter Four 35

Chapter Five 47

Appendix one..59

References..69

About the Author 71

Index... 73

CHAPTER ONE

A Sketch of The Utterson Road at Mary Lake

1868 See Reference(1)

John McAlpine was the first settler in Port Sydney. He built a log shack and also built the first saw mill on the east side of the present dam site.

David Hoagaboam then constructed a house and store where the Muskoka 10 makes a sharp bend and leaves the lake.

Ladells arrived and built west of Hogaboams.

The fifteen mile road from Bracebridge to Utterson was incredibly bad. At times it was impassible due to fires burning on either side. The air was hot and stifling. Here and there were fallen trees which had to be dragged out of the narrow road before the stage wagon could go on. The passengers became acquainted with and suffered from "corduroy' roads

Corduroy Road

Mr. Jos. Oliver was appointed resident agent and reported that there were 59 settlers between Lake Simcoe and High falls. Land was being sold for $1.00 per acre.

1869

A flood of settlers arrived that year including the following families: Jenners (who later established Clyffe House), Smiths, Kays, Kneeshaws, Browns, Theobalds, Osbornes, Hoths. and the Thoms,

William and Emilie Thoms

-**William Lawrence** and his family settled on land that included the Island named after him at the north end of the lake.

-**The first school** was built opposite the north end of Bridgedale Rd. and in c. 1882 SS #9 was opened across the road at Rosedale Apartments

SS#9

A settler's Cabin

<u>**Typical of the stories of these people**</u> is the one told about the Hoths as told by Mildred Hoth.- **See Reference(2)**

"September 1869, my father and mother landed in Montreal from England with five children.

We came by train to Barrie which was the terminal and then by boat to Washago. A stage took us to Gravenhurst and then by boat to Bracebridge. We were left there while my father and brother went on to locate land for our new home. A month later we left on foot and it took two days to get there. Mother had such a severe shaking up in the stage journey from Washago to Gravenhurst that she refused to make another trip that way Today it takes forty five minutes by car. When we reached Utterson we stocked up on provisions at Scarlett's Store and finally arrived at the Mary Lake end of the trail that is now the Utterson Road.

On either side of the trail was the unbroken virgin forest where the ring of the axe was yet to be heard. The only house was a hut occupied by John McAlpine. He made the first dam on the river. A large pine had fallen across the water and he drove stakes around it, banking it up with mud and stones.

McAlpine's Mill

Often as a little boy I watched him make his bread. He would open his bag of flour, pour in some water, add soda and mix it with his hands until the water had taken up as much flour as it could, then molding it into a flat cake to fit his frying-pan he would cook it over the open fire in the fireplace.

We crossed the river below the falls in a small dugout canoe called "the Man Killer" to stay in a small cabin owned by two young men from Scotland until our house was ready. The latter was 16x20 and boasted two small windows.

The first winter was not a hard one. There were no long stretches of cold weather, but the snow was 6 feet deep. Father made us snow shoes from split pine with rope lacings. He and my brother spent most of their time cutting down trees around the house.

About twice a week we would go to Utterson to the store for supplies carrying along bags which we would sling over our shoulders with the groceries. One hundred pounds of flour would be divided in half for my father and brother to carry. Nearly everything came in bulk and not in fancy packages like today.

I remember the bee that was held to cut out a rough road from Indian Landing to the Utterson Trail. This road was the foundation of the one that runs through the village today. My work was underbrushing. By noon we reached the big rocks on the crest of Town Hall Hill.

I shall never forget the first spring and the black flies and mosquitoes. We were absolutely unprepared for them. They came in clouds and as mosquito netting or screens were unknown, we were at their mercy. We were bitten so badly about the face and neck that it was impossible to turn our heads.

I recall going out with my sisters to the woods to collect moss from the trees. It came off in great sheets 3 inches thick. We brought home bags of it and it was pounded into the chinks of our log cabin and plastered over with clay so that no wind or cold could penetrate in the winter.

Muskoka Received its name from the Indian Chief Mesqua Ukee who had fought with the English in the Wat of 1812. Each fall would see the Indians with their families from the Rama reserve canoeing past our place making their way to their hunting and trapping grounds far up to the north. In the spring they came back laden with furs and pelts. Chief Bigwin and Menominee were chiefs among these tribes and I knew the latter quite well. He was a fine old man."

Chief Bigwin

The Story of The Kays

<u>Diary by Ann Kay - See Reference(3)</u>

"Saturday Sept 25th "Today we have quite a change in the weather. It is very cold. The people are very kind to us where we are staying, but it will not suit the "pocket" to stay here so we are going to rent a small house till father decides on his land.

Monday September 27 Today is fine and warm again. We ate in our new house now. Two young men have been living here this summer here but have kindly gone somewhere else that we might have this place. There is a large stove and they have given us the use of it for free. They stoves are invaluable appliances. You can boil five pots, a large wash boiler, and bake your bread all at the same time. Unfortunately we cannot get a boiler this winter. They cost too much. They want $30. for them. They are cheap at that. We shall get a three legged pot and have an open fireplace, put in bread and cover it all over with fire and let it bake. We shall have to put up with a few inconveniences.

A neighbour kindly lent us her washboard and we washed five dozen clothes in the time it would take to wash two dozen in the old style of rubbing with the hands. Yesterday one of the farmers killed a cow and today he sent Mother a bit for her breakfast weighing over ten pounds.

Monday October 4th Father came home last Thursday (Sept. 28th) from Stephenson. He has got 600 acres of fine land given to him. It is a few acres short of the 600 acres but that shortage is offset to him by a lovely river running through our land and we shall have a bridge over it next spring. There are thousands of cherry and nut trees on our land. They gave me 100 acres because I am over 18 years of age. Jim will spend his summer with us as every settler is compelled to live six months in every year on his land. Father and Will have gone to Stephenson to see about getting a house up for us."

"Anne's brother Alfred, who was 8 at the time, picks up the story.

"The first snow arrived that year on October 22 but by mid November the family had constructed a cabin 16' by 20'. The cabin had two windows which was a real luxury at the time. The family lived in this house for the first ten years and then moved to a new house a quarter mile up the river. The first house was abandoned because it was behind a hill and was in shadow a lot of the time. They were both called 'Inverness House' as a memory of their

Scottish background. William Kay who was 2 years older than Alfred made the two sketches of the houses about 1885

The First House

The Second House

"The Kay family cleared two acres of land that first summer, 1870. And with that small beginning the Kay farm prospered. The youngest son, Alfred, reported as follows:

The first crops were put in with a hoe and harvested with a sickle. We progressed to a scythe and grain cradles later. We sowed turnip seed on the newly burnt-over land and the dragged a small tree over the ground among the stumps to cover the seed. When we got our first yoke of oxen things were easier.

The second year we had a cow. Our hay was gone by December and from then until the spring the cow lived on the tender branches of the maple trees which the children gathered. We grew oats, peas, potatoes, turnips for our own use and when the lumber camps were established we could sell our produce to them for cash. My father who had been a postal clerk for thirty years before we left Scotland drew a monthly pension of about $1.00 a day as long as he lived. This pension was a big help to us."

Alfred Kay (**1861 – 1949**) He has written an autobiography of his life in Port Sydney. He became a self-taught taxidermist. Alfred's collection of one hundred and thirty six bird and mammal skins were given to the Royal Ontario Museum in Toronto.

CHAPTER TWO

1870 Robert Brown Family move to Muskoka. The First bridge is built across the river upriver from the present location.

1871 Richard, William and Joseph Clarke arrive from Udora. Allan McInnnes' family located in Brunel Township.

Albert Sydney Smith See Reference (4)

"Mr. Smith (as he was often called in Port Sydney)applied under the Free Land Grant Act for a lot which had been abandoned by a previous settler (McAlpine) and he also acquired three other lots which the same settler had held including a sawmill.

Mr. Smith made himself quite a deal. Old deeds show that he paid about $56. for 85 acres which today comprise almost the whole village of Port Sydney.

While he was Canadian by birth, he had been brought up in a home where the English tradition was strong. He saw himself becoming the squire of the district, Albert believed that there should be a village centred round his mill. He rebuild and enlarged his sawmill, and added a gristmill and oatmeal mill. These were designed to make Port Sydney a centre for the surrounding farms.

Sydney Smith's Home

Next came the lumbering boom. For the lumbermen, the principal prize was pine, which for years went down the river every spring both as squared timber and as saw logs." "When timbers were pouring down the river during the spring drives, enough stop-logs were kept in the sluice-way to raise the water and drown out the rapids.

The great days of lumbering were the years between 1870 and 1890. Albert Sydney Smith's mill used some 800,000 feet of logs a year.

To the end of his life he preserved one stand of virgin pine to the south of Port Sydney. A pathway through it was known as" the cathedral walk." After his death the new owner cut all the trees down for timber. It is known as Bridgedale subdivision today."

1872. **In 1872 a meeting of the settlers was called to choose a name** for the community and its post office. David Hoagaboam merchant, reeve of Stephenson Township, wanted the place to be called a port, and residents were agreed that Mr. Smith's first name should be used, so Port Sydney became the name. The post office was at Hoagaboam' s store.

-The first school which had been built opposite the north end of Bridgedale Road was abandoned. A new school was built in what is now the Robinhood Apartments.

The first Coloured Family Arrives See Reference(5)

The Story of Edward Enty

Edward was the grandson of Tobias Enty who originally came from the Caribbean.

"The records show that this inexperienced man(he was a cooper by trade) had a hard time building his house. He often told his neighbours that he would be more at home making an oaken barrel or wash tub but with the help of his neighbours, he soon had a cozy home.

The Enty House

"His wife was a motherly humanitarian type of person with a good knowledge of treatment of human ills. She was much sought after in their growing settlement that didn't have a doctor, and most folks couldn't have afforded one at that time anyway.

Like all early settlers, it was a hard life for them. The father's trade as a cooper was of little use to him here, where the demand was for lumber jacks who were skilled in taking out the pine logs that nature had so generously bestowed upon Muskoka. The closest store for the Enty's was in Port Sydney. When provisions were needed, Edward would walk that trail that the settlers used. He would instruct his wife to leave their cabin at approximately the same time that he would be leaving Port Sydney for the return trip. That way they would meet approximately half way from home. She then helped him carry the flour and provisions the rest of the way home. If wheat had to be ground into flour at the mill in Port Sydney, it meant that the heavy load had to be carried both ways. Unless a canoe could be borrowed. This of course was only possible in summer. In winter walking was the only way. This lasted until a road was cut out for wagon traffic."

Edward Enty died in 1905.

1873 **The Anglican Church** was erected at Port Sydney with a stone foundation being added in 1878. William Clarke and Emma Ladell were the first couple to be married in the Anglican Church.

The Anglican Church

Captain Cock settled on the point of land adjacent to his land holdings. When the lake levels rose inn 1878, he had to build a causeway to the shoreline.

Captain Cock's Home

Forrest Island Owners: Rumballs by land grant 1873 to 1889, Forrest and heirs 1889 until 1947. Aitken and Johnson from 1947onward.

William Duncan Forrest lived in the village from 1891 until the early 1900's. He was a bookkeeper for Sydney Smith during that period. He did not live on the island.

1873 -1877 The Locks at Huntsville are built
The water was raised six feet to operate the locks and to overcome the rapids that existed where the swing bridge was located in Huntsville.

1874 **A rough Road** was cut through Port Sydney from Indian Landing to the Utterson Trail by volunteer labour.

At the corner of Morgan Street and Muskoka 10, a **hotel** was built in the village by Wm. Morgan

Morgan's Hotel

1876 **The first Town Hall** was opened in Port Sydney at the top and west side of the rocky hill opposite the end of the dam. It was called the Music Hall. Fire destroyed the hall in the early 1890's.

Mr. Sydney Smith and Mrs. H. G. Ladell led the grand march to celebrate the opening of the Music Hall.

Robert Brown donated a plot for the first Stephenson Township Cemetery after the death of his daughter Mary.

The Northern was launched. **See Reference(6)** "The Northern was built and owned by Captain Alfred Denton. It was launched at Port Sydney in 1876 and was the first steamer on the North Muskoka Lakes. She had a hinged smoke stack to enable her passage under the original Huntsville bridge which did not swing until 1889. The Northern was 80' long by 24' wide. She carried passengers and freight to Huntsville and Hoodstown. The steamer was replaced by the Erastus Wiman which was built in 1890. The Northern spent her last days as a tug. She made her last trip in1893 and was dismantled in 1897".

The Northern at dock beside the Port Sydney Mill

Writer, actor and artist Charles Rumball See Reference(7)

"Charles was a man of many artistic gifts: a notable author and playwright, a splendid artist and cartoonist, singer, a rare narrator and a first class amateur actor. His passion, humour and love of the arts helped make Port Sydney the cultural centre of Muskoka in the 1870's and 1880's.

Port Sydney had the talent – singers, musicians, actors- and at the heart of this merry company of creative amateurs was Charles Rumball.

In the fall of 1871 Sydney Smith informed his friend Charles of the free land grants. As a result Charles, Kate and their four children arrived on the shores of Mary Lake.

Clearly the Rumballs were on the party circuit. In fact the settlers soon dubbed the Rumball homestead Hilarity Hall."

Hilarity Hall

They owned the island named Rumball Island as noted in the Bracebridge Land Registry Records. It was later called Forrest Island. On it they used to grow strawberries and watermelons.

In 1876, needing a place to display the village talent, he initiated the construction of the Music Hall. In the 1879 Guide Book and Atlas of Muskoka and Parry Sound Districts, Charles wrote that Port Sydney has a large public hall in which amateur dramatic performances are presented regardless of expense. He didn't mention that he was the principal actor, producer and director of these popular performances. In 1873 he was among the founding benefactors of Christ Anglican Church"

Charles died suddenly of a stroke on December 26, 1894, age 69. At the time he was the town clerk for Brunel Township, a position he held for four years. He is buried in the churchyard of Christ Anglican Church overlooking his beloved Mary Lake."

Charles Rumball

CHAPTER THREE

1877 The village had **a fife and drum band**. It was organized by Mr. Nichol as band master. They played in 1877 to celebrate the Northern's first trip.

The village also had a **Cricket Club.** Coleridge Roper was the captain and they played against Huntsville, Sisted and Bracebridge.

1878 Stone foundation was put under the Anglican Church

**A Christmas and Happy New
Year Card from 1878
Port Sydney 1878**

Season's Greetings

Port Sydney, on Mary's Lake, is a most charmingly situated Village. Here tourists can find a comfortable and well-kept hotel, whence may make most enjoyable boating excursions along the picturesque shores of Mary's Lake. The Anglican Church, in the village, a large gothic edifice, furnished with stained glass windows is a lasting monument to Rev. Mr Cooper, through whose exertions, mainly the church was built. Port Sydney residences, a large public hall, in which amateur dramatic performances are given with great effect and got up regardless of expense: also a grist mill, oat mill, and some good stores. It is reached from Huntsville in the summer by the "Northern" steam boat, and enjoys a triweekly mail from Bracebridge, with a daily mail stage in the summer.

-**The lake level** was raised about 6 feet by the new lumber dam in Port Sydney

-**An Atlas of Muskoka** was produced. It was called "Guide Book Atlas of Muskoka and Parry Sound District." It is still available.

1880 Cottrill's Mill Built See Reference (8)

"The dam at the locks raised the level of the water enough so that a mill was built there as well. At first it was operated by C.W Jacobs and by 1904 by Benj. Cottrill. The mill had a 56' diameter lumber saw and several other saws for trimming. To service the mill a small swing bridge was built across the trenched canal leading to the locks.

Logging was done in the winter and the logs were brought to the mill in log booms. They were mostly softwood logs because the hardwood logs tended to sink. By 1935 trucks were used to bring some logs to the mill. The MNR bought the mill in 1955 and gave the Cottrills until 1857 to salvage what they could."

Cottrill's Mill. The swing bridge can be seen in the background

1880 A bush fire swept through this part of Muskoka stripping trees from the islands and part of the village. Residents were forced to take refuge in the lake to avoid the flames.

Rocky Island and Crown Island
showing the results of the Fire

1885 Knox Presbyterian Church was built

Knox Church showing the drive shed at rear.

Allan McInnes and Rebecca Watson were the first couple to be married in the church.

1885 The Jenner Family Started to take in guests in what was to become Clyffe House

This was argueably the first of many lodges and guest houses. As lumbering production slowed down in the late 1800's, following the lead of the large Muskoka Lakes, lodges on Mary Lake began to take in guests from Toronto and nearby American cities. After another twenty years the guests began to build their own cottages and so the community gradually evolved from those days.

Clyffe House

Status of Hotels and Lodges

Name	Status
Arcadia House	torn down
Avon Lea	a private home
Flag Inn	an Inn
Grunwald	burned
Gryffin Lodge	a private cottage
MacInnes House	a restaurant
Marshall Cabins	unused
Mary Lake Inn	an apartment building
Mulvaney Cabins	unused
Muskoka Lodge	torn down
Nichol's campground	not in use
Pine Lodge	a lodge
Ridge Cove Cottages	operating
Riverside House	burned
Rosewood	an apartment building
Spruce Lodge	torn down
Sydney Hotel	burned
Victoria Villa	a private home

1886

-**The stone cottage** on Deer Lake Road was built

-**The first Lake Level problem** arose.

Report of the Commissioner For Public Works For the Province of Ontario (9)

"Complaints having been made to the Department that the lands of some of the settlers around Mary's Lake were injuriously affected by water, owing to the height at which it was necessary to keep it maintained in the early part of each season to serve navigation and lumbering interests."

"The outlet of the lake has been enlarged by the removal of an obstruction in the shape of a ledge of rock, and the dam has been extended by the construction of three piers, thus forming two additional stop-log openings."

"This dam is intended to facilitate the passage of saw-logs and timber down the river by retaining sufficient water on the rapids to float them over, without drawing the quantity from the lake which has heretofore been required to enable this obstruction to overcome."

-Port Sydney suffered a serious blow to its growth by being by-passed by the railway that went through Utterson on its way to Huntsville.

1890- 1905 the cheese factory operated. The steamer 'Gem' went around the lake to pick up milk cans for the cheese factory. The whey from the production of cheese was pumped across the river to a pig pen on the point.

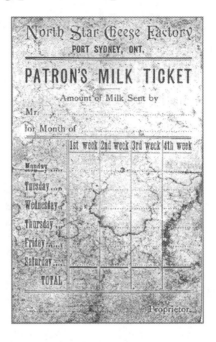

c.1895 **A shingle mill** was built at the east end of the beach. It operated until approximately 1904.

Mary Lake Inn

It started by a family called The Quigleys on land purchased from the Ladells to provide room and board for the workers from the shingle mill across the street. (Cedar shingles can still be found in the water around the beach) At the time the Inn was called Lakeveld, perhaps after the interest in the Boer War in South Africa. When George Cadieux bought it in 1920, the clientele was mainly summer guests. He called it View du Lac for a while but later changed it to Mary Lake Inn.

Mary Lake Inn c 1930

1897 See Reference (10) **The first Gem Steamer** was launched on the lakes. It was built on the flat area at the NE corner of the mill pond where Sydney Smith had built a marine railroad and repair shops. It collected milk for the cheese factory and carried passengers and freight. It was 35 feet long and when it burned in 1904 was replaced by 50 foot and later 53 foot Gems.

The first Gem shown with Sydney Smith on the dock

CHAPTER FOUR

1900 Appendix- See Reference(11) The Story of Victor Clarke's Life

A fascinating glimpse into the life of a person at the time. It can be found at the back of this book.

-The Olan Family (12) "moved from Perry Township near Novar to the Enty property. Here Alfred Olan (the father) learned the operation of the mill and in 1900 moved to the present site of MBC. He had plenty of help in running his mill there as his wife bore 15 children. The MBC land had been partially cleared by a family called Bacon.

At first Alfred located the Enty Mill, which he had purchased, on top of the hill at Muskoka Baptist Conference but later moved it closer to the river. By 1930 when MBC took over, the Olan's had extended their business to include not only the mill but also a lodge across the river called Breeze Point Tourist Home."

1900

-Bonner Island Formerly Stewarts Island was sold to Sydney Smith on April 2, 1900 and was registered with the Sheriff of Muskoka in 1923. The island does not appear to be named after any resident of Port Sydney nor was there any resident in Stephenson Township by that name at that time.

1905 First Annual Regatta

CanoeTilting
(Where the object is to knock the opponent out of his canoe)

A women's Team passing an egg on spoons

Regatta Day 1911)

1916 The Johnsons first come to Port Sydney
See Reference(13)

"Sydney Smith invited his nephew, the Rev. Herbert Johnson, his wife Bessie and their six year old son George to Port Sydney where they were put up in the cheese factory which Sydney owned. The family stayed there six summers and young George developed a life- long revulsion for cheese because of its rank smell brought out in the hot summer days."

The Cheese Factory from Johnson's Cottage

"In 1923 they had a cottage built by Arthur Clarke and Hugh McInnes on a lot donated by Sydney Smith on the west side of the river. Later George Johnson took time from his job at the Financial Post to publish an important book on the history of Mary Lake Pioneers called "Port Sydney Past" produced in 1960."

The Johnson Launch Called 'Old Girl"

1925 July 1 The Community Hall See Reference(14)was opened.

"Lying along the south shore of Mary Lake, the little village of Port Sydney has an air of knowing its own mind. It is no Johnny-jump-up among villages. It has its roots back to the days when they thought of comfort and charm first and what other people did a long, a very long time after. At the same time, it is very much in line with present thoughts and feelings— it boasts one of the finest community halls anywhere in the province."

The Community Hall

"This hall complete with public library room, kitchen. large stage, dining room in which 150 can sit down to dinner, screened casement windows and a perfect dancing floor, cost only $4300. Raising money for it was the joint effort of the Women's Institute and the Young People's Club."

Sydney Smith and Mrs. Jenner led the Grand Parade to open the new hall.

1931 Muskoka Baptist Conference See Reference(15)

"The young people from several churches in Toronto complained to their pastors that there was a real need for a camp where people with moderate income could blend recreation and Christian fellowship. In 1930, the first camp was held at Fisher's Glen near Port Dover. 134 campers from 32 churches attended. Accommodation was in tents and a rented hotel. The problems that arose were first: the hotel did not expect so many and the workers expected a raise for their work and secondly the temperature went down and they had to seek blankets from Brantford.

The result was the purchase of 117 acres at the present site along with 5 tourist cabins and three other buildings. 1931 was the first year and it brought many problems as described by DeLoss Scott, a handy man.... 1. The ride from Toronto with the car loaded to the roof with supplies. 2 The road into the camp—ugh.3 The condition of the camp. Grass and weeds everywhere to a height of about three feet. And the sleepless nights because if the mosquitoes. The old tumbledown barn where ten boys slept in the hay loft. "

"At first camp directors and staff occupied tents, meals were prepared in the kitchen of the old farm house and served on the wide verandah or in the newly constructed dining hall. Women and girls occupied five cabins on the river bank. Families and middle aged men occupied tents.

Directors and staff members not only served voluntarily, but often paid the full rate asked of guests.

There was plenty of variety in the programs of the camp. There were hikes to Blueberry Mountain, paper chases, treasure hunts, and tennis tournaments. Without the work of T.E Hurley which included countless practical details, the development of MBC would have been improbable if not impossible."

1933 The community of Port Sydney decided to spruce things up and so work crews **planted pine trees** along the Utterson road. This created the lovely entrance to the village.

1937 Crown Island. Owned by Dr. and Doris McMehen from Detroit. They were great friends of the Demericks who owned the Isle of Pines. They had a big log cabin and lots of gladiola gardens in rock gardens. The house eventually burned down.

House on Crown Island

The Caplins of Toronto bought it afterwards and held parties with their staff from their store.

Between the Wars Canon Pennington led a rifle club. Sessions were held regularly at a range at the back of Vic Clarkes lot and both men and women participated it it.

Canon Pennington is seen at the Lych Gate of the Anglican Church.

A Newspaper report in1937 states: "82 year old A.W. Clarke shot a perfect score at the recent match of the Port Sydney Shooting Club. Twenty shooters were participating. Results of the other members were G. Gowan 99, Stuart MacDonald 99, Vic Clarke 99, Mel Clarke 98, Bert McClure 98, J. Pennington 98, Sheriff Elliot 97 etc."

Muskoka Cyclone See Reference(16)

"Residents of this area, including a score of summer cottagers were today engaged in clearing away wreckage left by a cyclone that swept a path of destruction over an eight mile area.

One cow was killed by a falling tree, roofs of three barns were lifted and have not been found, a steel barn roof was found three quarters of a mile from its original base, cottages were twisted clear around from their foundations and others collapsed under the strain of the wind storm."

1939 Mary Lake Motors

In 1939 at the intersection of what was then Hwy 11 and the only road into and out of Port Sydney, the service centre must have been a busy place. The corner contained Grimes Garage, Ridley lodge, an information bureau and gas pumps.

Seth Grimes sold the property in1949 to Dalt Saunders but tragedy struck in 1953 when the building burnt to the ground, It was rebuilt on the same spot.

Mary Lake Motors

CHAPTER FIVE

-1847 Stephenson Township Central School System See Reference(17)

"The township was first thrown open for settlement in the early 1860's. It was not until 1870 that the first school was opened at Parkersville and that was designated as school section #1.

Strange as it may seem none of these schools were of log construction but in general were of frame construction. All were heated by wood stoves and lighted by coal oil lamps; to their last days they were heated by wood. These buildings are still standing some serving as residences. The oldest of these schools were built without any government help."

SS#9 Port Sydney

"It was these schools which had been in service for 70 years that the Department of Education felt should pass out of existence as schools. They did not now measure up to the standard for educational services.

About 1944 a school area was organized in the Township of Stephenson including the village of Port Sydney to establish a consolidated school. A meeting was called and attending it were Dr. Althouse, Director of Education and Dr. Greer, Superintendant of Elementary Education for Ontario. They directed the Board of Trustees to purchase the property for a consolidated school.

Despite shortages of building materials because of the war, particularly nails, the school was opened in September 1 1947. It was called the

VK Greer Memorial School and was opened by the Honorable George Drew, Prime Minister of Ontario.

The most exasperating experience during this period was the problem of convincing settlers to accept the dismantling of four schools each of which was considered part of their local community. It took one year of steady pressure to get them to accept it."

Retiring Teacher: Children Good See Reference(18)

"Forty Years as a teacher have convinced Miss Hilda Clarke of Port Sydney that most youngsters are good and develop into worthwhile citizens,

She expressed the opinion during the weekend when residents of the village paid tribute to her with a surprise party at VK Greer Memorial School. She retired from the school at the end of her fortieth year of teaching.

Her faith in teens was reaffirmed the previous year when she accompanied a busload on a trip to Expo at Montreal. "They were really wonderful" "

1946 Cavalcade of Colour Starts

Starting in 1946 the Cavalcade of Colour lasted until the 1970's. The following communities belonged to it. Bracebridge, Port Carling, Port Sydney, Huntsville, Gravenhurst and Bala. Each community hosted the affair over the years.

The planning committee held regular meetings over each winter. There was talk of having a holiday in Muskoka on the day of the Cavalcade. Newspapers in Toronto and even National Geographic was contacted. It was promoted at the Sportsman's Show and other groups like car rally's were asked to participate. Kodak was involved in photo tours; signage was set up for tours.

The week of the Cavalcade was topped off with a grand parade and show at one of the communities. The Cavalcade of Colour was a great success. It was a way of promoting Muskoka and getting visitors to our area.

Bracebridge's Pipe Band Led the Parade

A Beauty Contest was a Highlight

The 1960 and 70's

The ski hill

The hill behind the Community Hall had all the possibilities of a ski hill. It was steep and even had jumps. All that was missing was the ingenuity to open it up. It lasted until the upper parking lot was expanded and the hill was destroyed.

A rope tow got people up the hill

The Hill

Dice on Ice

From 1957 until about 1963, an event called Dice on Ice was held in March on the lake. It was another attempt by the village to bring tourists to the community in the long winter days. Local drivers competed against drivers from all over the area. The ice was plowed into a track...and they were off!

1963 Snowmobiling See Reference(19)

"Wilfred and Ross Clarke brought the first snowmobile to Port Sydney in 1963. It was an autoboggin that had the 7 horsepower engine in the back with no brakes and just a throttle.

It came from a dealer in Parry Sound and they tried it out along the gas pipeline and up the ski hill behind the village hall."

An Autoboggin

"Jack VanAlstine was convinced to become a dealer and by the end of the winter there were four autoboggins in the village. They would go through three or four feet of snow with no trouble and if they got stuck even though the machines weighed about three hundred pounds the riders did not worry much about the weight.

By 1965 there were enough snowmobiles around and enough people interested in them that a club was formed. At first it was called the Port Sydney Snowmobile Club. Later that got changed to the Hill and Gully Riders because a man from Utterson after riding over the nearby hills said, "You guys are just a bunch of hill and gully riders."

Back in those days they mostly rode through drifts and along old logging trails. When the trails got rough, they used to drag bed springs behind them to level the trails. Riding on the lake was a pleasure. The winter carnival started about that time and so they held snowmobile races at the carnival. A feature that was a lot of fun were the treasure hunts organized by the club."

An expedition by the club

"No one knew about the lakes back in from the roads except maybe trappers. The snowmobiles opened up these lands. It was like discovering and opening up new vistas."

When the Federation of Ontario Snowmobile Clubs was organized Vera VanAlstine became the first secretary and from her kitchen table wrote memberships for all of Ontario.

The Beast Feast

For several years the community held a Beast Feast. The local hunters would all contribute meat that they had shot or trapped to a dinner held at one of the local lodges. The meat would be prepared by the hunters and there was a good natured competition among them to make their presentations as succulent as possible. The whole community enjoyed this feast.

Isle of Pines

For several years in the 80's and 90's the Isle of Pines hosted a music night. Boats full of people would anchor off the south end of the island and listen to a live music presentation by the owner.

Clouds

Across the rippling lake,
Beyond the island necklace,
Rising imperiously over manicured hills,
Cascades of billowing clouds drift,
Sun-dipped to slate shades commingle
Creating shifting phantom shapes
Or bodies in postures of repose,
Allowing mortal thoughts to float,
A fleeting escape from reality
And day-to-day anxieties
That ambush and snare our dreams.

By Eleanor Kidd

APPENDIX ONE

A SHORT STORY OF VICTOR CLARKE'S LIFE
As told by
LAURA CLARKE

The old farmhouse still standing on Lot 24, Concession 8, was my place of birth on May 24 1900. My father Arthur William Clarke of Ireland, was the grandson of and Irishman who fled the potato famine in Ireland and eventually settles in the Udora are of Ontario. My mother, Ada Marie Osbourne, was a school teacher and grandmother and missionaries from England. The Osbourne family went to the west Indies and later settled in Parkersville, Muskoka.

I was the eldest of eleven children, all but one surviving. Audrey, my eldest sister, was also born at the farmhouse. In 1904 the family moved to the site of what is now the Village Inn. At first we lived in a small cabin by the cedar tree while dad built the Belleview Lodge. This took longer than was expected because deep snow in 1904 made hauling the logs out of the bush impossible.

Belleview Lodge

Finally, the Belleview opened for business on June 28th, 1906 with tourists coming from the cities by train into Utterson. We also served meals to tourists coming from Huntsville by way of the steamship Ramona. The boat stayed overnight and made two round trips from Huntsville per day.

I remember rowing over to Clyffe House with Audrey to pick berries for my mother in the blueberry marsh in the area where the Bridgedale subdivision is now. We sold 11 quarts to the Clyffe House for $1.25 and brought the second 11 quarts home. We also picked strawberries around that area and Blackberries where the pipeline is now on the Addison Farm. My brothers Mel, Dalton, Murray and sisters Hilda, Iva, and Alma were born while at Belleview. Dalton died at the age of 18 as a result of the flu epidemic. We attended school in the building which is now part of the Robinhood Apartments. Mrs. Edith Cadieux was my last school teacher in the fall of 1915. Since the war had started, I had to quit school and go to work as the men were scarce.

About 1917 my parents sold the Belleview to the Lumbers family and moved to lot 23, Concession 7 where the Schell's live now. My sister Wanda and Marie and brother Ross were born at the family house. The Lumbers used the Belleview as a private home.

The Clarke House

James Lumbers started a sheep ranch which my father, A.W.Clarke, managed. The ranch was built on Lot 23. My job was to feed the sheep twice a day. My friend Alvin Marshall and I took a rail fence and went into the bush to cut cedar posts and for that work we were paid 75 cents per day. Of course, I still worked at home and have memories of helping dad to bring home sugar and groceries from the local store in trade for eggs and butter.

In the spring of 1919 I bought my first car, a touring Model T. Dad picked up tourists at the Utterson station in a bus he converted from a Ford one ton truck. In 1913 he got into the taxi business in a big way – charging 50 cents from Utterson and $2.00 for a round trip from Huntsville – of course we only paid 25 cents a gallon for gas in those days.

Dad's taxi

In 1920 I took on a job for Stan Hanes who was in lumbering. In the winter the horses and sleighs would take 17 loads of logs per day from Utterson to Mary Lake. I was hired as a guiper and had to level log roads ready for watering so the sleigh's runners wouldn't get stuck. In five weeks we moved 25000 logs. I never laid my eyes on my boss but I must have done a good job as he hired me again to move tanbark from Mud Creek to the Utterson freight cars.

In 1922 I met Orah Cowan from Hamilton who was at that time a guest at one of the tourist houses known as the MacInnes House. We were married that year and I started building the house I now live in.

In December 1922, I walked with my dad through a foot of snow to Utterson to vote in the provincial election. I voted for Will Hamill of the United Farmer's of Ontario, the party which joined Mackenzie King's Liberals to form a government. This government was the first ever to advertise tourism in Ontario.

There were a couple of winters when work was scarce in this area. In 1922 I took a job with Hamilton Wood Products. Then in 1928 three other fellow from Port Sydney and I went to Hamilton again and worked at the Thistle Club. During most winters in the 20's, I managed to get work cutting wood and ice. Bob Jenner at Clyffe House paid me to provide ice for his refrigerator where he hung his meat for the summer guests.

Vic Clarke cutting ice at the Town Dock

In the early 1920's I had gone into the taxi business. One of my memorable fares was a trip to Sprucedale when my car broke down. My fare and I hiked into Sprucedale and hopped a train home to get my dad to come and tow the car back. It was 4 am before I got to bed that night. My dad and I kept up the taxi business for some years and often went to Toronto to pick up cottagers. After the Dionne quintuplets were born there was quite a call for us to drive tourists to Calladar and North Bay to visit their home. In the 1930's cars became common and the taxi began to peter out.

In 1925 my father had the job of building the Community Hall and I helped along with other volunteers from the village. That year the ice didn't go out of the lake until May 12th and it froze every night. We had the shell of the building up by June1st and the temperature rose to 90 and 100 degrees fahrenheit every day so we had to start work on the roof at 4 am to beat the heat.

I remember my parent's raising money for the Community Hall by holding chicken dinners at their home. The guests would eat in the downstairs of the house and dance upstairs.

The year 1930 sticks in my mind for cutting Christmas trees. Two weeks before Christmas we had 30 inches of snow and then on December 23 we had 30 inches more! This sure made work difficult. On Christmas Day it started to rain and didn't stop for two weeks. We never got any more snow that winter and only had ice left.

As well as the taxi business and building houses, I used to look after caretaking for cottages. I had five widows and two maiden ladies who depended on me to look after their property.

Sadly in 1931 Orah died and it wasn't until 1933 that I met Laura Jennings. Laura was attending Shaw's School of Business in Toronto but had not found work and so was working at Muskoka Lodge for the summer. She and the other girls used to row over to Port. I was close at hand one night and invited Laura to the ice cream parlour which was located in the present post office. I continued to see her that summer and we got married in October.

By 1934 we had decided to take in tourists, so we enlarged the present house and built two cabins. We called the tourist house "Victoria Villa" and stayed in the business for twenty years. We had our own garden and built a hen house and had laying hens to provide us with eggs. One summer we rented a cow from a local farmer for our milk and cream and paid him $2.50 a week for the cow plus pasture. Of course, we only got $12.50 per week for room and board from our guests.

Victoria Villa

Looking back, my life was not all work. We went on trips with friends to Ottawa and Northern Ontario. I manage to get away hunting as far as Port Loring. We took off time to go trolling for lake trout in Mary Lake as we had our own boat house and boat. We went to Florida twice, in 1965 and 1966, with Marion Grimshaw and her husband.

Over the years, I served on the school board, Chamber of Commerce and the Mary Lake Association. I helped to negotiate the purchase of land from Sydney Smith at Indian Landing and the parkland from Mr. Hoth, both for the Village.

Since my retirement from building in 1976, I have managed to keep pretty busy with the garden and helping Laura with her quilting. Over the years we have made many, many quilts both for gifts and for the church and this has kept us both busy.

Life has been good to me and I feel fortunate to have good health. I will be 91 on May 24th,1991·

REFERENCES

1. from hand written notes by Hilton Brown

2. from Pioneer Days at Port Sydney p 27- 32

3. Diary of Ann Kay – provided by Michael Ball

4. Albert Sydney Smith from a newspaper article by Stanford Dingman

5. The Story of the Entys by Joe Cookson

6. The Northern Steamboat Huntsville Public Library

7. From the 'Master of Hilarity Hall' an article written for The Muskokan May 27 2011 by Judy Laberge, great granddaughter of Charles Rumball. She is the Author of "The Rumball Family, Pioneers in Port Sydney, Muskoka", available in the Bracebridge and Huntsville public Libraries.

8. from talk given by Craig Olan in 1993

9. From the Commissioner for Public Works For the Province of Ontario 1886

10. from a letter by George Johnson to Bill Clarke

11. A Short Story of Victor Clarke's Life by Laura Clarke

12. from a Newspaper Article 1987 by Susie (Olan) Chantler

13. from a letter written by Ted Johnson 2011

14. from a newspaper article in the Globe and Mail 1930

15. from an article called The Beginning of Miracles

16. from an article in a local newspaper

17. from an article called "Stephenson Township Pioneer Central School System"

18. from an article in a local newspaper called Retiring Teacher: Children Good

19. From an interview with Bill Clarke

ABOUT THE AUTHOR

Ryan Kidd is a retired teacher and administrator. He and his wife Eleanor, who was also a teacher, poet and edited all his books, have lived in Port Sydney for twenty six years. He is currently active in the Mary Lake Association. He was elected Citizen of the Year in 2007. In 2000 he developed a self-directed Historical Walking Tour of Port Sydney and in 2003 co-authored "These Memories I leave to

You" with Dave Scott. That book describes the settlers around Mary Lake. In 2011 he wrote "The Newcomers" which describes Mary Lake from 1870 - 1940.

This current book portrays personal stories and photos of the resolute people who established Port Sydney.

INDEX

A

Albert Sydney Smith 13, 15, 69
Allan McInnnes' 13
Autoboggin 55

B

Beast Feast 57
Belleview Lodge 59, 60
Bonner Island 36
Brown 13, 21, 69

C

Canon Pennington 43, 44
Captain Cock's 19
Cavalcade of Colour 50, 51
cheese factory 31, 34, 38
Chief Bigwin 8
Clarke 13, 18, 35, 38, 44, 49, 54,
        59, 61, 62, 64, 70
Clouds 58
Clyffe House 3, 29, 60, 64
Corduroy Road 2
Cottrill's Mill 26, 27
Crown Island 28, 42, 43

D

Dice on Ice 53

E

Edward Enty 16, 18

F

Forrest Island 19, 23

H

Hilarity Hall 23, 69
Hoagaboam 2, 15
Hoth 4, 68

I

Isle of Pines 42, 57

J

Jenner 29, 40, 64
Johnsons 37

K

Kay 9, 11, 12, 69
Knox Presbyterian Church 28

L

Ladells 2, 33
Lawrence 3
Locks 19

M

Mary Lake Inn 30, 33
Mary Lake Motors 45, 46
McAlpine 1, 5, 13
Morgan's Hotel 20
Muskoka Baptist Conference
       35, 40

N

Northern 21, 22, 25, 26, 67, 69

O

Olan Family 35

P

Port Sydney v, vii, 1, 12, 13, 14,
       15, 17, 18, 20, 21, 22, 23, 25,
       26, 31, 36, 37, 38, 39, 42, 44,
       45, 48, 49, 50, 54, 55, 64, 69

R

Rosedale Apartments 3

Rumball 22, 23, 24

S

school 3, 15, 47, 48, 49, 59, 61, 68
shingle mill 32, 33
SS #9 3
Sydney Smith 14, 19, 21, 22, 33,
       34, 36, 37, 38, 40, 68

T

The Anglican Church 18, 26
The Community Hall 39, 40
Thoms 3
Town Hall 7, 21

U

Utterson 1, 2, 5, 7, 20, 31, 42, 56,
       60, 62, 63, 64

V

VICTOR CLARKE 59
Victoria Villa 30, 66, 67

Printed in the United States
By Bookmasters